God's
little book of
Love

Words of joy and delight
for caring souls

Richard Daly

Collins, a division of
HarperCollins Publishers
77–85 Fulham Palace Road

First published in Great Britain in 2007
© 2007 Richard Daly

Richard Daly asserts the moral right to be identified as the author
of this work

A catalogue record for this book is available from the British
Library

ISBN-13: 978-0-00-724623-6

10 9 8 7 6 5 4

Typeset by MATS Typesetters, Southend-on-Sea, Essex
Printed and bound in Great Britain by
Martins the Printers Ltd, Berwick upon Tweed

CONDITIONS OF SALE

This book is sold subject to the condition that it shall not, by way
of trade or otherwise, be lent, re-sold, hired out or otherwise
circulated without the publisher's prior consent in any form of
binding or cover other than that in which it is published and
without a similar condition including this condition being imposed
on the subsequent purchaser.

All rights reserved. No part of this publication may be reproduced,
stored in a retrieval system, or transmitted, in any form or by any
means, electronic, mechanical, photocopying, recording or
otherwise, without the prior permission of the publishers.

INTRODUCTION

Love – what an endearing word. It has been the
basis for so many poems, songs, speeches and
prose. Through love human relationships are born,
and it is the golden cord that keeps people
together. It is indeed love that
'makes the world goes round.'

However, what happens when love for one another
is withdrawn, and the power of its effect reduced?
It is disastrous, for we cannot survive without love.
Yet could it be that we are actually seeing the
evidence of this today?

Is love for one another being eroded, in our
society? I think many may conclude that the
answer is yes, but that does not have to be the
situation with you. Each of us have the seeds
of love, and they can be cultivated
to grow and spread to each other.

You can make a difference, even if it is only
in the life of one person.

This volume is designed to provide a wealth
of ideas and thoughts to help you make
a positive difference in somebody's life.

Richard Daly

KNOW GOD, KNOW LOVE
NO GOD, NO LOVE

'He that loves not, knows not God,
for God is love.'

1 John 4:6

LOVE IS SEEING

True love does not come by finding the perfect person, but by learning to see an imperfect person perfectly.

Proverbs 10:12

MAKE A SACRIFICE OF LOVE

Showing compassion demands dying
to self-interest.
It disrupts well-ordered lives,
it costs us money,
it calls for time,
it means making sacrifices –
it involves laying down your life for others.

John 15:13

PUT OTHERS FIRST

Be blessed, by blessing other people.

Matthew 5:14

FEAR NOT

'There is no fear in love,
but perfect love casts out fear.'

1 John 4:18

LOVE IS LIFE

The grandest moral and ethical goal of humanity
means nothing without love.

1 Corinthians 13:1

REST IN THE ARMS OF GOD

In extreme assaults of stress
God invites us to rest in his eternal embrace.

Matthew 11:28

LOVE'S GREATEST GIFT

Through God's great love Christ was treated
as we deserve, so that
we can be treated as he deserves.

John 3:16

YOU'RE NEVER FORGOTTEN

One of the most breathtaking concepts of scripture
is the revelation that God knows each of us
personally, and that we are constantly
on his mind day and night.

Psalms 8:4

GOD'S LOVE HAS NO BOUNDARIES

There is simply no way we can fathom the extent of God's love for us. As the song says, it's so high you can't get over it, so wide you can't get around it, so low you can't get under it.

Psalms 139:1-2

AN UNCONDITIONAL LOVE

God continues to love us even when we don't
feel the same towards Him.

Romans 5:8

GOD'S ON YOUR CASE!

Never assume that God is silent or inactive simply
because it seems we do not hear from him.
Be assured, he is silently working on your case.

Psalms 37:34

YOU'RE NEVER ALONE!

The Lord doesn't always solve our problems
instantly. Sometimes he permits us to walk through
the 'valley of the shadow of death.' But he is there
with us, even in our darkest hours. We can never
escape his endless love.

Psalms 73:23
Psalms 23

CAST YOUR CARES ON HIM

God hears the faintest cry of the sick, the lonely,
the bereaved and the depressed of the world.
He cares deeply about each one.

Psalms 40:1

AN EVER-PRESENT FRIEND

God's heart is tenderly drawn towards the
downtrodden and the defeated. He knows your
name, and sees every tear.

Psalms 34:18

BE COMFORTED

'The Lord is close to the broken-hearted,
and saves those who are crushed in spirit.'

Psalms 34:18

THE SILENT PROTECTOR

We will never know how often the Lord
quietly protects us, directs or leads us.
He is an ever-present companion.

Psalms 46:1

ONLY TRUST HIM

When we submit to the will of the Lord we can say
with confidence that in all things God works for
the good of them who love him, who have been
called according to his purpose.

James 1:17

NOT OUR TIME, BUT HIS

While God's purposes and plans are different
from ours, he is infinitely just,
and his timing is always perfect.

2 Samuel 7:28-29

FROM TEST TO TESTIMONY

God wants to use the lessons from your
experiences of adversity, to encourage others
going through the same thing.

Genesis 12:2

TO KNOW GOD
IS TO EXPERIENCE HIM

It's during those periods where your faith has been
challenged that you get a better understanding of
who God is, and the extent of his love.

Psalm 91:4

WATCH YOUR MOODS

Establish your spiritual foundation not on
fluctuating emotions but on the authority of God's
written word. God's love never changes.

Malachi 3:6

LET GO, LET GOD

We are assured in scripture that we are never left
to fight our battles alone. That is great news
for all who are weary and burdened.

1 Samuel 17:47
2 Chronicles 20:15

SPREAD LOVE

'As I have loved you,
so you must love one another.'

John 15:12, 17
Hebrew 13:1

PUT FIRST THINGS FIRST

'I may have all knowledge, and understand all secrets. I may have all the faith needed to move mountains – but if I have no love, I am nothing.'

1 Corinthians 13

BE A CONQUEROR

'Who shall separate us from the love of Christ?
shall trouble or hardship or persecution or famine
or nakedness or danger or sword?
No, in all these things we are more than
conquerors through him who loves us.'

Romans 8: 35–37

HE'S GOT YOUR BACK!

God's love for us is a protective love. He says, 'He that touches you, touches the apple of my eye.'

Zechariah 2:8

YOU ARE PRICELESS

The price paid for us was imaginably high – the
blood of Jesus Christ. Now we belong to him.
That ought to put a smile on our faces.

John 3:16,17
1 Corinthians 6:20

LOSING TO WIN

We often think of love as giving, but sometimes
love involves taking away something
that would not be best.

Job 1:21

AVOID THE MYTH

Contrary to popular opinion, God doesn't sit in
heaven with his jaws clenched, hand in a fist
and a deep frown on his face.

Exodus 34:6,7

LAY DOWN YOUR BURDENS

Our problem is that we hold on to our worries and anxieties. The Bible says 'Cast your cares upon him, for he cares for you.'

1 Peter 5:7

GOD IS WHO YOU NEED HIM TO BE

In God we have a Lord and a shepherd: a Lord who can place a hundred billion stars in space, who is so mind-numbingly mighty; yet who can come to us as a shepherd and touch us with the gentleness of a mother's hand.

Psalms 23:1

MAKE THE CHANGE

What's blocking you from experiencing God's love? Find out as soon as possible, and refuse to live another day without that love in your life.

Roman 5:5

TURN IT OVER TO JESUS

What matters to you, matters to God. There's no
problem so insignificant that he doesn't want
you to tell him about it. What's important
to you is important to God.

Hebrews 13:22
Hebrews 13:5

LET GOD LEAD

If you believe that God has a unique plan for your
life and loves you unconditionally, you will
abandon yourself to Him in trust, knowing that
in the end 'all will go well' for you.

Jeremiah 29:11

EXPERIENCE FREEDOM

Whatever you refuse to forgive, you relive. It robs
you of the joy of loving and of being loved in
return. Unforgiveness is an umbilical cord that
keeps you tied to the past. When you forgive,
you cut that cord.

Ephesians 4:32

THERE'S HOPE FOR YOU

You who have been abused, abandoned, betrayed,
or feel as if you never measure up: God says to
you, 'I have loved you with an everlasting love;
I have drawn you with loving-kindness.
I will build you up again.'

Jeremiah 31:3,4

RISE TO THE CHALLENGE

Loving others does not mean much if we only love
the people we choose to, based on our terms and
conditions. But loving those who are different from
us in personality, culture, race, and loving them in
spite of their difference is the real challenge!

John 13:34

RELEASE YOUR POTENTIAL

Jesus does not penalise us for our past, or label us.
Knowing the worst about us, he still sees the best.
That's what he expects us to do for others, too!

Ephesians 5:2

CHOOSE TO LOVE

Love is a choice, not a mood, a magic feeling
or a reaction, but a choice.

1 Peter 2:4
Isaiah 43:1

WORSHIP IN SPIRIT AND TRUTH

Our worship to God ought to be a total
expression of our gratitude and praise to the one
who loved us when we were hopeless, destitute,
lonely, fearful. Who filled us with his peace,
wrapped us in his own identity, and gave us a
place of honour.

Psalms 113:3

ESTEEM OTHERS HIGHLY

Never let your own suffering blind you to the
needs of those around you. Jesus was more
concerned with other people's needs than his own.
We should take our cue from him.

Philippians 2:3,4

BE A VESSEL OF LOVE

God is looking for people he can use as a vessel to
reach out to love other people. Will you be one?

2 Peter 2:21

FROM SELFISH TO SELF-LESS LOVE

Modern thinking says 'I'll love you if you meet my needs.' That's selfish. True love focuses on the needs of the other person.

Ephesians 5:25-27

TRUE LOVE PART 1

'Love is patient and kind, never jealous or envious,
never boastful or proud, never haughty or selfish
or rude. Love does not demand its own way.
It is not irritable or touchy. It does not hold
grudges, and will hardly ever notice
when others do it wrong'.

1 Corinthians 13:4,5

TRUE LOVE PART 2

When you love someone you will be loyal to them
no matter what the cost, you will always believe in
them, always expect the best, and always stand
your ground defending them.

1 Corinthians 13:6,7

LOVE THE UNLOVING

Avoid the trap of self-righteousness, and act with
humility and grace when you encounter someone
whose lifestyle makes you uncomfortable. Begin to
see them not through your preconceptions but as
someone loved by God, and in need of the
same grace you received.

1 John 4:8

VALUE YOURSELF, VALUE OTHERS

Good marriages, relationships and friendships are all based on Christ's golden rule. 'Whatever you want someone to do to you, do also to them.'

Matthew 7:12

LOVE IS A LASTING JOURNEY

Against popular opinion, Love doesn't
'make the world go round':
Love is what makes the ride worthwhile.

Song of Solomon 8:7

LEARN FROM YOUR PAST

Every experience you have had, from the moment you were born until now, has made you who you are today. Use these experiences to cultivate your love.

Romans 8:28

A WORD OF AFFIRMATION

One of the most beautiful passages in scripture is
found in Isaiah: 'You are mine. When you pass
through the waters, I will be with you. When you
walk through the fire you will not be burned; you
are precious and honoured in my sight. I love you.'

Isaiah 43:1-4

TO BE LOVED, LOVE

Our attitude toward others determines their
attitude towards us. Smile at people
and they will smile back. Show acts of love,
and they will reciprocate.

Proverbs 23:7

BE TRANSFORMED BY LOVE

God likes to take the lost, the least and the lowest and make something beautiful of them. If you feel like you are one of the above, let God do what he likes to do best and make you an object of beauty.

Isaiah 1:18

CHECK YOUR MOTIVES

True love will never ask of a person anything that
will devalue them, or disassociate
them from God's will.

Philippians 4:8

RESPECT YOUR LOVED ONE

If 'God is love' the reverse must also be true:
'love is godly.'

Amos 5:15

DON'T BE FOOLED BY FEELINGS

Someone said, 'Love is a feeling you feel when you feel you're going to feel something you've never felt before.' Fortunately, real love doesn't depend on just feelings.

1 Corinthians 13:7,8

LOVE IN THREE WORDS

Many poems have been written and many songs
sung, all trying to define the one word, love. One
dictionary uses 27 words. The Bible defines it in
just three, 'God is love.'

1 John 4:6

WITH GOD, YOU CAN'T LOSE

God's love to us is unfailing – your name is
engraved on the palm of his hand. He knows you
better than you know yourself, your sins of
yesterday and of tomorrow are before his eyes; yet
the verdict is still, 'I love you.'

Psalms 103:11

MEMORIZE JOHN 3:16

This verse is perhaps the greatest expression of love ever: 'For God so loved the world, that he gave his only begotten son, that whosoever believes in him should not perish, but have everlasting life.'

John 3:16

LET LOVE CHANGE YOU

Some think, 'If I try, I can change my partner.'
Don't use your love to try to change your partner,
use your love to change yourself!

Romans 12:3

WAIT ON HIM

'And we know that in all things, God works for the good of those who love him, who have been called according to his purpose.'

Romans 8:28

BE THERE

When someone is hurting, the most loving thing
to do is simply to be there. Though you have
nothing to offer except your presence, that
speaks louder than words.

2 Corinthians 1:4

LIVE UNSELFISHLY

Give without expecting in return, forgive even though you are not forgiven. Share, though no one says thank you. This is love in action.

Luke 6:35

IT'S OK TO LOVE YOURSELF

To love yourself is not about pride, but an
appreciation of who you are in Christ. Before we
can love others, we have to learn to love ourselves.

Matthew 22:39
James 2:8

LOVING CAN BE DIFFICULT

The greatest sacrifice we make is choosing to love
those who are not easy to love.

Matthew 5:44

Luke 6:27

BE CHILDLIKE

Children have a natural way of spontaneously
expressing their feelings of love. If there's any
virtue in regression, that could be it.

Mark 10:15

LOVE NEVER ENDS

The fact that love never fails, means it never gives up, nor permits itself to be hindered or defeated by evil. It is constant, immovable.

Jeremiah 31:3

KEEP GOD'S LAW

The Ten Commandments can be summed
up in one word – love. Love for God, and love
for our neighbour. God says, if you love me,
keep my commandments!

1 John 5:2
John 15:10

GUARD AGAINST SELFISHNESS

By nature, we are often 'takers'. Biblical love
involves making a conscious decision to be 'givers',
asking 'What can I do to serve you?' rather than,
'What's in it for me?'

Philippians 2:3

ACCEPT THE RAIN, AND SHINE

A love that is 'enduring' weathers the storm of life.

Psalms 107:29
Isaiah 25:4

LOVE CONQUERS ALL

'There is no difficulty that enough
love can not conquer;
no disease that enough love will not heal
no door that enough love will not open
no gulf that enough love will not bridge
no wall that enough love cannot bring down!'

Emmet Fox

Romans 8:37

SEE YOURSELF AS LOVABLE

Much happiness is achieved when there's the
conviction that you are loved in spite of yourself.

Proverbs 10:12

GIVE LOVE, GET LOVE

'If you want to be loved, love and be loveable.'

Benjamin Franklin

Romans 13:8

EXPRESS LOVE CREATIVELY

There are many inexpensive ways to tell the one
you love how much you care – write a poem (it
doesn't have to rhyme), plan a surprise lunch, hide
love notes around the house. Be creative!

Song of Solomon 4:1-16

GET READY FOR A SURPRISE

'No eye has seen, no ear has heard,
no mind has conceived,
what God has prepared for those who love him.'

1 Corinthians 2:9

EXPRESS YOUR LOVE TODAY

The revealed instinctive desire of many when facing
death is to call a loved one, to say 'I love you'.
But why wait until such a crisis?

Song of Solomon 7:10

MAKE A COMMITMENT

True love is not a feeling by which we are
overwhelmed. It is a thought-out decision, by
which we are committed.

Psalms 18:1

LOVE YOUR ENEMIES

It is natural to love those who love us. It is supernatural to love those who hate us.

Proverbs 8:17
Hosea 14:4

AN IMPARTIAL LOVE

There is nothing you can do to make
God love you more. There is nothing you can
do to make God love you less.

John 15:13

LET CHRIST FILL YOU

By its nature, human love is conditional. Only through Christ in us can we produce *agape* (unconditional love), only he can fulfil us in joy, peace, and compassion.

2 Corinthians 5:14

A MOTIVE OF LOVE

'It is not how much you do, but how much love
you put into the doing, that matters.'

Mother Teresa

Psalms 17:17

LOVE SEEKS NOT ITS OWN

'Love consists in desiring to give what is our own
to another, and feeling that delight as our own.'

Emanuel Swedenborg

Micah 6:8

CREATE A LOVING ATMOSPHERE

Every house where love abides and friendship
is a guest, is surely a true home.

Mark 3:25

SEIZE THE MOMENT

'I shall pass through the world but once, any good
that I can do or act of kindness, let me do it now,
let me not deter or neglect it, for I shall
not pass this way again.'

Stephen Grellett

Psalms 118:24

CHERISH LOVING MEMORIES

Nothing can erase those precious moments
of love known within your life. These treasures
belong to you, and are to be cherished for
the rest of your life.

Psalms 105:5
Song of Solomon 1:4

ENJOY YOUR LIFE

'The more you give, the more you get
The more you laugh, the less you fret
The more you do unselfishly
The more you live abundantly.'

B Kent

Luke 6:38

BE BLESSED TO BLESS

Each of us has been entrusted with certain gifts
to steward for each day. Let us use them well; life
is ours for such a brief span of time.

Matthew 5:16

PRAY WITH LOVE

If love is the greatest force in the world, and prayer
the mightiest force in the world, then when we
pray in love we are working with a power
that can move the world.

James 5:16

REMEMBER THE GOLDEN RULE

Show love to others, as you would have them show
love to you. This is the golden rule of love.

1 John 4:19
John 15:12

WATCH YOUR REFLECTIONS

Life is like a mirror: if you frown at it, it frowns back. If you smile, it returns the greeting.

Galatians 6:7

GET RID OF HATE

'When Jesus said "love your enemy", he meant every word of it. We never get rid of an enemy by meeting hate with hate. We get rid of an enemy by getting rid of enmity.'

Martin Luther King

1 John 4:18
Luke 6:27

THE ESSENTIAL INGREDIENT

What is important in life is knowing how
to give and receive love.

1 Peter 2:17

CLAIM YOUR INHERITANCE

As God's beloved child, you are a member of the
royal family of the king of heaven. You are highly
esteemed and greatly honoured. You are an heir to
God's kingdom, and have direct access to the
throne room of God. You're royalty!

1 Peter 2:9

LOVE'S NOT A FAIRYTALE

A truism of love is that it ends happily ever after –
yet true love has no ending.

Psalms 34:12

GROW IN LOVE

Contrary to popular belief, we never 'fall' in love,
but 'grow' in a greater understanding and
appreciation of what it really is.

2 Peter 3:18

LOVE SEES ALL

Love is not 'blind': it sees more, not less, but
because it sees more, it chooses to see less.

Romans 5:8

DON'T BE DECEIVED

Many people confuse infatuation with love.
One is a temporary, changing emotion, the other
is a giving, permanent, principled decision.
Don't be fooled!

Proverbs 17:17

LOOK FOR THE OPEN DOOR

When the door of happiness closes, another door
opens. However, often we look so long at the
closed door that we don't see the one
which has been opened for us.

Revelation 3:8

SEE THROUGH THEIR EYES

Always put yourself in others' shoes.
If you feel them rubbing at you painfully,
they probably hurt them too!

Romans 12:14-21

LEARN TO BE PATIENT

To love someone is to let them just be themselves,
and not to seek to change them into our own
image. Otherwise we love only the reflection of
ourselves we find in them.

Philippians 3:21
1 Corinthians 15:51

BE CONTENT

The happiest people don't necessarily have the best
of everything, they simply make the most of
everything that comes their way.

Hebrews 13:5
Philippians 4:11

EXPRESS APPRECIATION

Never miss an opportunity to let those who are
essential to your life know how much you love,
appreciate, and think of them each day.

Ephesians 5:20

JUST ONE WORD FOR LOVE

We say we love our spouse, our children, and in the same breath we say that we love fried eggs. Don't let language confuse your understanding.

1 John 4:7

LOVE CAN DO WONDERS

'I love you not only for what you are,
but for what I am when I am with you.
I love you not only for what you have made
yourself, but for what you are making me.'

Ephesians 4:15

LET GOD FILL YOUR EMPTINESS

We all have a void in our lives that needs to be
filled with love. Often human love falls short of
filling this, but this void can be filled through the
love of God. Open your heart to him today.

Ephesians 3:19

BOUGHT WITH A PRICE

A high price was paid by God to show his love for us. Through Christ, that love is freely available.

Hebrews 12:2

WHEN LOVE HURTS

When we love someone, we take them into
our hearts. That is why it hurts so much
when we lose someone we love – because
we lose a part of ourselves.

Revelation 21:4

AVOID POSSESSIVENESS

'Possessive' love cannot be true love at all: in fact,
it is an act of selfishness. Love ought to respect a
person too much to dominate them.

John 5:42

LET GOD REPAIR THE HURT

Have you been let down by someone you love?
Jesus is 'very close to the broken-hearted, and very
near to those who are crushed in spirit.'

Psalms 34:18

LEARN FROM CHILDREN

Learn to express your love freely and without
inhibition. Take a lesson from children:
they do it all the time.

Matthew 19:14

COVER HATRED WITH LOVE

Hate has a reason for everything.
But love is un-reasonable.

Amos 5:15
Luke 6:27

FOLLOW YOUR INSTINCTS

The moment a child is born, their natural instinctive need is for love. When death stares you in the eyes, the last natural instinctive need is love.

Isaiah 66:13

SOFTEN UP!

No matter how tough people's exterior may be,
we all need to love and to be loved.

Romans 5:5

KNOW YOUR REASON FOR LIVING

There are three questions of value in life.
What is sacred? What is worth living for?
And what is worth dying for? The answer
to each is the same: only love.

John 15:13

GIVE TO RECEIVE

Love is quite something: if you give it away,
it comes right back to you.

Matthew 10:8
Luke 6:38

NEVER FEEL YOU'RE UNLOVED!

What motivates you to live another day? It must be
love. What motivates you not to want to live
another day? The false perception that you are not
loved. But God always loves you!

2 Peter 3:9
John 3:16

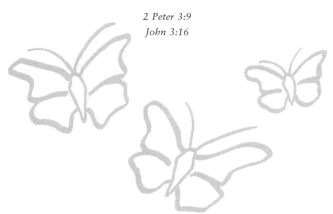

YOU DESERVE IT

Those who need to be loved the most,
are those who deserve it the least.

Luke 7:47

GIVE HOPE TO A LIFE

If someone tells you that 'nobody loves them',
endeavour to prove them wrong.

Genesis 4:9

BE AMAZED BY GRACE

The amazing thing about God's love for
us is that he accepts us just as we are!

Psalms 103:10
Roman 4:7

DON'T NEGLECT YOURSELF

If we are committed to loving others, we must also treat ourselves with the same love.

John 3:2

ACCEPT GOD'S FORGIVENESS

Forgiveness is a fruit of love. And it also involves
learning to forgive ourselves.

Psalm 91:1-13

CONFESSION IS GOOD FOR THE SOUL

When a person accepts the forgiveness of God,
they are exposing themselves to the greatest
therapeutic power in the world. It could save years
of physical and spiritual illness.

Luke 23:34
Luke 6:37

GIVE IT UP

By handing over your problem to God, we can
experience the power of emotional release, a very
real enhancer of the immune system.

Psalms 55:22

UNSTOPPABLE

'Many waters cannot quench love.'

Song of Solomon 8:7

BE FAITHFUL IN LITTLE THINGS

One source of happiness is to find time to make
one small act of service each day. Only those who
love to give, have really learned to live life.

1 John 3:18

BE OPEN-MINDED

We all need to learn not to be quick to judge,
or quick to condemn.

Romans 14:13

HUG SOMEONE TODAY

Hugging is all natural. It's organic, naturally sweet,
no pesticides or preservatives. No artificial
ingredients and 100% wholesome.
Doesn't that sound nutritious?

Romans 12:9,10

THINK LOVELY THOUGHTS

'Whatsoever things are true, whatsoever things
are lovely – think on these things.'

Philippians 4:8

WRITE A LOVE LETTER

Expressing your love to someone in writing allows
you to choose the choicest words that reflect the
inner sentiments of the heart. Once inscribed,
it can be treasured for life.

Job 19:23
Proverbs 3:3

READ HIS LOVE STORY

The Song of Solomon contains the most loving
descriptive passages. Read a passage today,
and get some tips.

Song of Solomon 4:1-5

MEDITATE ON NATURE

Look around you: there are hundreds of ways in
which God is telling you how much he cares.
He says, 'Be still and know that I am God.'

Psalms 46:10

STORE PRECIOUS MOMENTS

Loving memories always bring a welcome smile.
By creating such moments today, you'll always
have something to look back on.

Psalms 139:17

BE A SOURCE OF HOPE

Giving is the secret of a healthy life – not
necessarily giving money, but encouragement,
sympathy and understanding.

Deuteronomy 1:39
Deuteronomy 3:28

MAINTAIN YOUR FRIENDSHIPS

True friendships do not come by chance. Each one
is infinitely precious. They are a source of life's
lasting joys, so appreciate them.

Proverbs 17:17

ONLY ASK

As long as it draws you closer to him rather than
pulling away, whatever you need, if you trust God,
he will supply it.

John 14:13
Luke 11:9

SPEND TIME ALONE

There are great benefits to be had from a time of
solitude. A brief hour on your own before
returning to the world relaxed and refreshed.

Psalms 23:2

LET CHILDREN SEE LOVE IN YOU

Give your children a home wherein
Love's fires are lit and never grow dim.
A place where children may always know
That they with their pleasures
and troubles may go.

Psalms 127:3

ONE FAMILY

If God is our heavenly father, and we are his children, that makes us equal. We are all brothers and sisters of the same one family.

Galatians 3:28

LEAD BY EXAMPLE

Making children feel loved and wanted is the primary aim of all parents. The simplest and most direct way to do this, is to tell them so, many times, day after day.

Proverbs 22:6

TRUST IN PRAYER

Prayer is the answer to every problem in life.
It puts us in tune with divine wisdom, which
knows how to adjust everything perfectly.

Luke 18:1
1 Timothy 2:8

CHOOSE YOUR MOOD

It takes no greater effort to be happy everyday
than it does to be miserable.

Proverbs 16:20
Proverbs 3:13

SEND AN ENCOURAGING CARD

What can dispel thoughts of despondency better
than receiving a letter from a friend?
What we write can say so much.

Luke 1:1–4

BE HOPEFUL

'Yesterday is always a dream
Tomorrow is only a vision
But today well lived
Makes yesterday a dream of happiness
And tomorrow a dream of hope.'

Kalidasa

Matthew 6:25–34

LET TODAY BE YOUR DAY

Today is your day and mine,
so let us search for the lovely things.

John 16:24

LET GOD HEAL YOU

In truth it is difficult to love someone who has
caused you much hurt and pain. In such a case,
present yourself to God to heal those wounds
so you can love again.

Matthew 5:11,12

LIVE TO LOVE

To live is to love, and to love is to live.

1 John 4:16

LOVE TO BE LOVED

If you wish to be loved, love.

1 John 3:17,18

GIVE YOURSELF

Love, above all, is the gift of oneself.

James 1:17

THE GREATEST OF ALL

'And now these three remain: faith, hope and love.
But the greatest of these is love.'

1 Corinthians 13:13

DON'T RUSH AHEAD

We live in a fast paced world where we have come
to expect instantaneous results. God doesn't
operate that way: he is not bound by our time.

Acts 1:7

SEEK HIS RIGHTEOUSNESS

'Every work of love brings
a person face to face with God.'

Mother Teresa

1 Corinthians 13:12

FIND A SECRET GARDEN

A beautiful garden is a peaceful spot where you can stop to reflect and catch a glimpse of life's deeper meaning. Visit one today, and be enthralled.

John 18:1

LOVE IS...

There are many metaphors for love.
Yet no human words can really define it.

1 Peter 1:8

ALWAYS GIVE A POSITIVE WORD

One way of experiencing love is through receiving
compliments. Yet they are 'biodegradable': they
dissolve over time after we receive them. That's
why we can always use another.

LOVE GIVES VITALITY

When you think you're in love, you don't go off
your food; on the contrary, your appetite
for good things is enhanced.

Song of Solomon 2:10-17

LOVING WHEN IT'S NOT RECIPROCATED

Giving someone your love is not an assurance that they'll love you back. Don't demand love in return, wait for it to grow in their heart. If it doesn't, be content that it's growing in yours.

John 15:18
1 John 3:13,15